First published in Belgium and Holland by Clavis Uitgeverij, Hasselt – Amsterdam, 2017
Copyright © 2017, Clavis Uitgeverij

English translation from the Dutch by Clavis Publishing Inc. New York
Copyright © 2018 for the English language edition: Clavis Publishing Inc. New York

Visit us on the web at www.clavisbooks.com

Firefighters and What They Do (small size edition) written and illustrated by Liesbet Slegers
Original title: *De brandweerman*
Translated from the Dutch by Clavis Publishing

ISBN 978-1-60537-384-3

This book was printed in May 2018 at Nikara, M. R. Štefánika 858/25, 963 01 Krupina, Slovenia.

First Edition
10 9 8 7 6 5 4 3 2

Firefighters
and What They Do
Liesbet Slegers

Clavis

NEW YORK

Fires are dangerous!
They must be put out quickly.
Putting out fires is the firefighter's job.
"Hello? Can you come right away?"
asks the person on the phone.

ring,
ring!

The firefighter wears a special suit.
It protects against heat and flames.
Doesn't the helmet look cool?

the visor
covers the face

helmet

light

visor

neck flap

gloves

coat

pants

boots

The firefighter rides in a firetruck.
He fastens the firehose to the fire hydrant.
An axe and rope hang from his belt.

hello
chief!

firehose

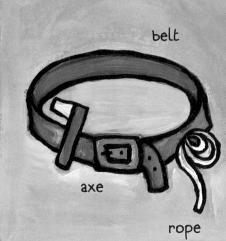

belt

axe

rope

fire truck

fire hydrant

Everyone is on duty at the fire station.
The firefighters slide down the pole.
It's faster than the stairs!

fire station

They put on their special fire suits.
First the pants and coat, then the helmet.
Heavy boots and gloves.
And don't forget the walkie-talkies!

quick!
get ready!

The siren blares.
Everyone out of the way!
Here comes the fire truck!
The chief rides in a separate car.

WOO-WOO-WOO

The fire hydrant is on the sidewalk.
Quickly, the firefighter attaches the firehose.
Now there's plenty of water to put out the fire.

The chief uses the walkie-talkie
to talk to the firefighters.
He tells them exactly what to do.
The firefighter on the ladder
sprays water on the roof.
The others spray water from below.

well done!

Whew! The fire is out!
Luckily, the house is still standing.
On to the next task.
The siren is off now.

saved!

Oh no! The car can't get through.
There's a tree down, blocking the road.
Is this a job for the fire department?

The firefighters pull the tree off the road
with a cable.
The driver can keep going.
"Thank you! You're my heroes!"
waves the driver.

Help the firefighters!

Which one needs to be put out?
The tree, the sun or the house?
Use your finger to follow the hoses.
Which one leads to the fire?

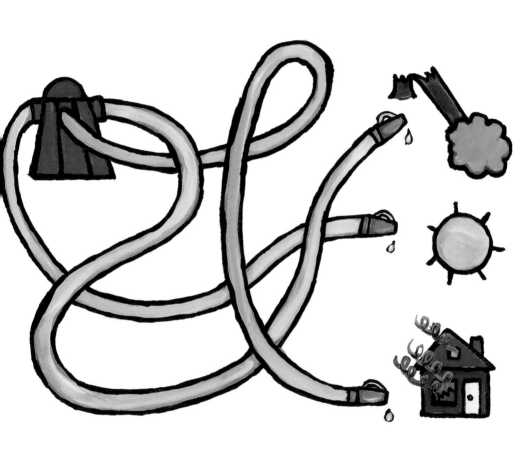